TODAY'S TOP DRIVERS

MAX VERSTAPPEN

BY KATE MIKOLEY

Gareth Stevens
PUBLISHING

HOT TOPICS

Please visit our website, www.garethstevens.com. For a free color catalog of all our high-quality books, call toll free 1-800-542-2595 or fax 1-877-542-2596.

Library of Congress Cataloging-in-Publication Data

Names: Mikoley, Kate, author.
Title: Max Verstappen / Kate Mikoley.
Description: Buffalo, New York : Gareth Stevens Publishing, [2024] | Series: Today's top drivers | Includes bibliographical references and index.
Identifiers: LCCN 2023013703 | ISBN 9781538287231 (library binding) | ISBN 9781538287224 (paperback) | ISBN 9781538287248 (ebook)
Subjects: LCSH: Verstappen, Max–Juvenile literature. | Automobile racing drivers–Netherlands–Biography–Juvenile literature. | FIA Formula One World Championship–Juvenile literature.
Classification: LCC GV1032.V47 M5 2024 | DDC 796.72092 [B]–dc23/eng/20230407
LC record available at https://lccn.loc.gov/2023013703

First Edition

Published in 2024 by
Gareth Stevens Publishing
2544 Clinton St
Buffalo, NY 14224

Designer: Tanya Dellaccio Keeney
Editor: Kate Mikoley

Photo credits: Series background Merydolla/Shutterstock.com; cover, pp. 1, 14, 22, 23 cristiano barni/Shutterstock.com; p. 4 Abdul Razak Latif/Shutterstock.com; pp. 5, 7, 19, 21 (top), 25, 27 motorsports Photographer/Shutterstock.com; p. 9 Action Plus Sports Images/Alamy Images; p. 11 PHOTOMDP/Shutterstock.com; p. 13 MrSegui/Shutterstock.com; p. 15 Ivan Garcia/Shutterstock.com; p. 17 https://upload.wikimedia.org/wikipedia/commons/d/dd/Podium_2017_Malaysia.jpg; p. 21 (bottom) Gregory Reed/Shutterstock.com; p. 29 Jens Mommens/Shutterstock.com.

Printed in the United States of America

CPSIA compliance information: Batch #CS24GS: For further information contact Gareth Stevens, New York, New York at 1-800-542-2595.

CONTENTS

A YOUNG STAR

Before he even won a Formula 1 (F1) race, Max Verstappen had made a name for himself in the sport. At just 17, he became the youngest person ever to race in F1. It wasn't long before he was scoring points and winning races too!

IN THE FAST LANE

Formula is a kind of car racing loved around the world. The cars have just one seat, open wheels, and an open **cockpit**. Formula 1 is the top class of formula racing.

MEET MAX

Max Verstappen was born on September 30, 1997, in Belgium, a country close to France and Germany. His dad, Jos Verstappen, used to be an F1 driver. His mom, Sophie Kumpen, raced a small type of race car known as a kart or go-kart.

JOS VERSTAPPEN

IN THE FAST LANE

Max's mother is from Belgium. His father is from the Netherlands. Even though Max is from Belgium, he races for the Netherlands.

A SPEEDY START

Many race car drivers got their start driving karts. It's a way for kids to get used to being behind the wheel. Verstappen was no different. As a teen, he won many karting **championships**. He won both European and worldwide titles.

IN THE FAST LANE

Verstappen won more than 20 karting championships.

FAST IN FORMULA

In 2014, Verstappen made his way into formula racing. He drove in the FIA Formula 3 European Championship **series**. He won 10 races and came in third place in the championship. That year he also joined the Red Bull Junior Team.

IN THE FAST LANE

In 2015, Verstappen joined another junior team owned by the company Red Bull, an F1 team called Toro Rosso.

F1 FIRSTS

Verstappen made history at his first F1 race. Only 17 years and 166 days old on the day of the 2015 Australian **Grand Prix**, he became the youngest person to ever race in Formula 1 to date.

IN THE FAST LANE

Two weeks after his first F1 race, Verstappen checked off another record. He became the youngest person to score points in an F1 race.

In 2016, Verstappen moved up from Red Bull's junior team to its regular racing team. In his first race with the team, he made history yet again. This time he was the youngest driver to win an F1 race!

IN THE FAST LANE

Verstappen was 18 years and 228 days old when he won the 2016 Spanish Grand Prix and became the youngest F1 winner to date.

CRUISING ALONG

Verstappen finished the 2016 season in fifth place. He continued to do well in the next few seasons, gaining a few more first-place finishes and several podiums. In 2019, he finished the season in third place, his best F1 standing yet.

IN THE FAST LANE

In racing, the podium is where drivers stand when they come in first, second, or third place in a race. When a driver finishes in one of these places, it's called "a podium."

In 2020, Verstappen again finished the season in third place. Of the 12 races he completed that year, he finished on the podium all but one time. He came in first at the Abu Dhabi Grand Prix and the 70th **Anniversary** Grand Prix in England.

IN THE FAST LANE

Verstappen was named Dutch Sportsman of the Year in 2016, 2021, and 2022.

AN F1 CHAMPION

The 2021 season was easily Verstappen's best yet. But he wasn't the only one having a great year. Before the final race, the Abu Dhabi Grand Prix, Verstappen had already won nine races. But fellow driver Lewis Hamilton had won eight.

LEWIS HAMILTON

IN THE FAST LANE

Before the 2021 Abu Dhabi Grand Prix, Verstappen and Hamilton were tied in points.

The 2021 F1 season came down to that last race. Verstappen and Hamilton weren't about to let it be a boring one. Hamilton led for most of the race, but on the last lap Verstappen passed him, winning the race and the championship!

IN THE FAST LANE

Some people didn't think the Abu Dhabi results were fair. A **safety car** had been called near the end of the race, which some said may have changed the results.

No matter what your thoughts were on the 2021 season, it was clear that Verstappen was a great driver. He proved that again when he won the championship a second time the next year. In the 2022 season, he won a record-breaking 15 races!

IN THE FAST LANE

Verstappen took part in 22 races in 2022. He won all but seven!

OFF THE TRACK

When he's not racing in a car, you might find Verstappen racing on a screen. He's taken part in several video game contests playing racing games. He has also worked with several charities, or groups that help those in need.

IN THE FAST LANE

In 2021, Verstappen put his own car up for sale to give money to a charity that helps people whose ***spinal cords*** *have been hurt.*

WHAT'S NEXT?

Known for both hard work and natural talent, Verstappen seems to have a bright future ahead of him. He won the first F1 race of the 2023 season, the Gulf Air Bahrain Grand Prix. It seems likely we'll see plenty more wins from this young driver!

IN THE FAST LANE

Verstappen was named Laureus World Sportsman of the Year in 2022. The award is said to honor the greatest and most inspiring people in sports.

TIMELINE

SEPTEMBER 30, 1997

VERSTAPPEN IS BORN.

2014

HE DRIVES IN THE FIA EUROPEAN FORMULA 3 SERIES.

2015

VERSTAPPEN BECOMES THE YOUNGEST PERSON TO DATE TO RACE IN F1.

2016

VERSTAPPEN BECOMES THE YOUNGEST DRIVER TO DATE TO WIN AN F1 RACE.

2021

HE WINS HIS FIRST F1 CHAMPIONSHIP.

2022

VERSTAPPEN WINS THE F1 CHAMPIONSHIP AGAIN.

FOR MORE INFORMATION

BOOKS

Arnéz, Lynda. *Be a Pro Race Car Driver.* Buffalo, NY: Gareth Stevens Publishing, 2024.

Olson, Ethan. *Max Verstappen.* Mendota Heights, MN: North Star Editions, 2023.

Rule, Heather. *GOATs of Auto Racing.* Minneapolis, MN: SportsZone, 2022.

WEBSITES

Max Verstappen
www.redbullracing.com/int-en/drivers/max-verstappen
Read more about Verstappen here.

Max Verstappen – F1 Driver
www.formula1.com/en/drivers/max-verstappen.html
Check out Verstappen's F1 driver page.

Max Verstappen Stats
www.espn.com/racing/driver/_/id/4665/max-verstappen
Find Verstappen's latest race results on his ESPN page.

GLOSSARY

anniversary: A yearly date marking a notable event.

championship: A contest to decide an overall winner.

cockpit: The place where the driver sits.

grand prix: One of a series of international car races.

inspire: To cause someone to want to do something.

safety car: A car that limits the speed of other cars on a racetrack during a caution period such as a crash or bad weather.

series: A set of events or races that go together.

spinal cord: A thick rope of nerve tissue extending from the brain.

INDEX